Excell
PDT
Professional Driving Training

*What You Always Wanted To Know
About Driving In Snow*

Excell
PDT
Professional Driving Training

*What You Always Wanted To Know
About Driving In Snow*

Guide for Passenger Vehicles

JOE MARTIN

Printed in the United States of America
ISBN 978-1-958434-59-8 (sc)
ISBN 978-1-958434-60-4 (e)

2022.11.10

MainSpring Books
5901 W. Century Blvd
Suite 750
Los Angeles, CA, US, 90045

www.mainspringbooks.com

Excell PDT
Professional Driver Training

Everything You Need to Know
About Driving in Ice, Snow, and Rain

Author Bio

When I reflect on my life—I am a son, husband, father, and grandfather—I need to acknowledge that I would have been a better disciplinarian if I had connected all the dots between learning and good decision-making. I would have made better decisions if I had made these connections sooner. I could have been a better father and husband if I had been more of a teacher than a disciplinarian—more concerned with teaching about behaviors and decisions that promoted positive results than just following rules.

Discipline offers two choices: the high road or the low road. Taking the high road in life is choosing to learn about which choices result in good decisions, bringing rewards. On the other hand, when one makes a low road decision, he makes decisions from a lack of understanding or incorrect information, which results in undesirable consequences and thus requires correction and limits potential.

My goal in writing this booklet is to help others make good decisions by providing them with the knowledge I have gained from 35+ years of driving all sorts of vehicles in all types of weather and on all kinds of road conditions. What I have learned from my own mistakes has allowed me to teach others what to do and what not to do. Additionally, I have the classification of "Expert" in controlling my vehicle in ice and snow and snow chain installation. I taught snow chain installation, anchor braking, and correct braking at Caltrans in Kingvale, CA, and I am one of only a handful of drivers in the nation who can haul off a 22% grade.

One mistake contributing to my desire to help others happened when I was employed as a "log truck" driver for Emmett Baugh Co. We were doing a winter job transferring decked logs from Oroville, CA, as high winds and severe rain moved in. I unloaded at Trinity River Lumber Co. in Weaverville, CA, and my semitrailer was empty as I was returning to the yard in Anderson, CA.

The conditions were heavy rain, low visibility, and high winds. I was only traveling thirty miles per hour at the bottom of Buckhorn Summit. I had been warned that I had an oncoming vehicle traveling toward me with its high beam headlights on. The vehicle was parked right before a right-hand turn by a rock wall bank with minimal shoulder and a two hundred yard drop to a creek.

Even though the rain had suddenly stopped like shutting off a faucet, there were about three inches of rain on the road surface. As I neared the other vehicle, I noticed that the vehicle was parked in a manner that blinded me as I got closer to the corner. I moved over to the left (I felt like I was driving by Braille) and gently stepped on the brake. When my peripheral vision came back, I could tell I would impact the rock wall. I quickly steered to the right and tried to stop.

However, I broke loose, causing oversteering problems, also known as spinout, which I could not recover from. I did not have the time or space to correct these problems, and the back of my log truck hit the rock wall. The impact tipped me over, resulting in a scalp laceration and an injured wrist and shoulder that I required surgery. Afterward, I studied the wreck, and the lesson I learned was the Degree of Fault Law, which emphasizes the importance of driving at a speed to stop at half the distance I can see.

Years later, I studied driving on ice and snow and learned about disruptive motion and multiplying forces. I learned that the following four forces contributed to my accident: low visibility, low surface grip due to loss of traction, and steering while braking.

As part of this painful and tragic lesson, I learned never to multiply forces. I was blessed to survive that accident and thankful to learn a hard lesson from it that I can now share with you, my readers.

Note: Everyone must own their own mistakes to learn from them. Over my 35+ years of driving, I have learned the difference between a wise man and a fool—a wise man uses the knowledge he has access to, and a fool does not.

My goal in writing this manual is to help professionals and the public improve their driving knowledge and skills so they will all reach their destinations safely.

Happy trails and happy reading,

Joe Martin

Interstate 81 in Pennsylvania in March 2022
YouTube: https://youtu.be/gkfwzJYUFIo

This YouTube video involved many different propulsion systems: Front-Wheel, 2-or-Rear-Wheel, All-Wheel, 4-Wheel, trucks pulling campers, and tractor-trailers. A failure to train drivers properly costs lives and billions of dollars every year. **Failing to train is training to fail**.

The accident resulted in five fatalities and involved over 50 vehicles during a snow squall on Interstate 81 in Pennsylvania in March 2022. One witness on the scene described the snowfall as being nearly white-out conditions. Yet when one observes the accident on the YouTube video, one can see the accident was due to the vehicles' high speed, improper braking, panic braking, and limited visibility, not white-out conditions.

Drivers should not be afraid to drive in snowy conditions, but they must respect the extra precautions that ice and snow require. Failing to train people how to control their vehicles on ice and snow can result in high prices. Finally, road surfaces can be hazardous at any time of year; therefore, the driver must be vigilant for conditions, especially snow, ice, fog, high winds, and wet road surfaces.

I recognize four contributing factors in this chain reaction accident in March of 2022.

1. Driving too quickly
2. Not braking correctly on ice and snow
3. Panic braking
4. Overdriving visibility

The Value of Discipline & Laws

Discipline is training yourself or others to obey rules or a code of conduct. Additionally, discipline requires punishing disobedience. In the case of a driver, a ticket, or worse, an accident, is a punishment to correct the noncompliance. Bad decisions have consequences that require correction. Limiting potential as opposed to good discipline is training that enables one to make good decisions that have a positive result, increasing the potential for opportunity.

Driving is a discipline because it requires training, good behavior, and constant exercising of good decisions. Good discipline enables the student to do a common thing uncommonly well. Driving is also a privilege afforded to those who train well and make good decisions.

As stated earlier, discipline offers two choices—the high or the low road. Taking the high road in life is choosing to learn about what choices result in good decisions, which will bring rewards. On the other hand, when one chooses the low road, one decides to make decisions from a lack of understanding or incorrect information that results in undesirable consequences and thus requires correction and limits potential.

High Road > > > Good Decisions > > > Positive Results > > > Potential Opportunity

VS.

Low Road > > > Bad Decisions > > > Consequences > > > Correction > > > limited Opportunity

Selective compliance —choosing which rules one will obey—is dangerous for everyone. Laws exist for the protection of everyone. Individuals cannot pick and choose which laws suit them. The law of motion neither lies nor changes. If people learn the laws and obey them, they can avoid consequences that require correction.

Bad Decisions

While driving, everyone makes hundreds of decisions. Some of the decisions are good, and we arrive at our destinations safely. While other decisions are wrong and inhibit our progress and possibly even take our or others' lives.

Some of the worst decisions people make are decisions driven by emotions. Every day, we see these decisions: speeding, disregarding traffic signs and signals, and not being patient and courteous on the road. Emotional choices often lead to selective compliance or picking and choosing what laws drivers will follow and what laws they will ignore or break. Selective compliance is always a wrong decision that bears with it undesirable consequences.

However, being aware of and choosing to maintain control over emotions will keep all drivers safe. Think about road rage for a moment. Road rage is simply a choice to be offended, which leads to anger, resulting in bad decisions requiring correction and limiting potential. Unsound choices based on emotions while driving are becoming too frequent.

A driver should not and cannot afford to be offended by others. Choosing to be offended leads to anger and more bad decisions. A driver must decide to remain calm or pay the potential consequences.

Basic Physics

The more a concept is understood, the more the concept will be used. Therefore, let's look at the science behind surface grips. Think of the word *friction* as *traction*. Kinetic (moving) energy is subject to the laws of motion. Therefore, a vehicle will remain in constant motion along a straight line unless acted upon by an internal and external force. Kinetic energy is the energy an object has because of its motion.

The three qualities of kinetic energy are as follows:

1. Energy always moves in the direction of travel.
2. The effect of energy when a vehicle takes a corner is to transfer weight, causing the vehicle to lean or roll over.
3. A skid mark results from kinetic energy exceeding the tire's surface grip. A skid mark translates into wheels locking up, spinning out of control, and losing control on the road.

How do drivers control kinetic energy? They minimize the forces or factors that contribute to the kinetic energy.

The Great Eight Forces or Factors Everyone Must Know

The first two are external forces; the next six are internal forces:

1. Road surface
2. Wind
3. Deceleration (braking)
4. Over Acceleration (too much fuel)
5. Steering
6. Weight transfer
7. Aggressive downshifting
   (manual transmission)
8. Engine brake or high-compression engines

Antilock braking systems or ABS brakes have helped prevent locked brakes, but they have not solved the problem. The only proper solution to the problem is to educate the everyday driver and the professional driver.

Ignorance comes at a higher cost than education. In compromised weather and road conditions, panic braking or slamming the brakes cause a loss of vehicle control because the tires will lock up. One should never slam on the brakes on ice, snow, or rain, for such an act violates the first law of motion, which says the body remains at rest or in uniform motion in a straight line acted upon by an external force.

Understanding these forces or factors is critical to safe driving in snow, ice, or rain.

Surface Grip Graph

Vehicles never really begin to have an adequate surface grip until they put steel on the ground, "traction control." See the graph below provided by the National Safety Council to understand better.

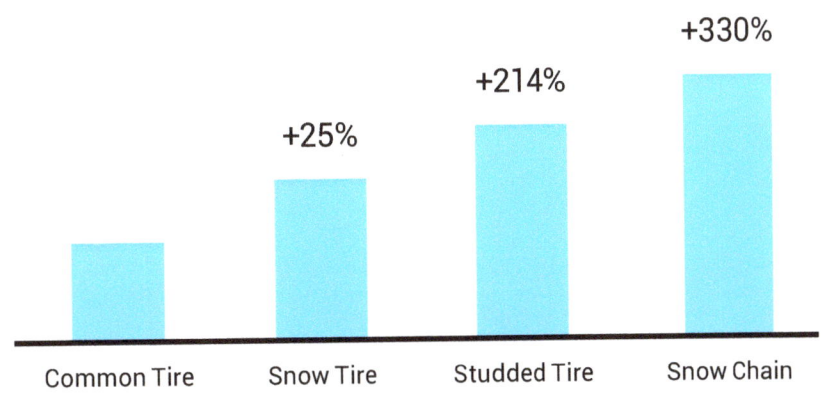

Factors a Driver Can Control

Speed

The greater the energy, the harder it is to control weight transfer, especially with light, short vehicles. A car requires a greater stopping distance when ice or snow comes into the picture. Ice and snow affect the amount of friction on road surfaces and impact acceleration/ deceleration. Ice and snow can disrupt motion.

Weight Transfers

Weight transfer happens when a car's weight moves around its roll center when braking, turning/cornering, or accelerating/decelerating. When the vehicle moves in one of these directions, the car's weight moves in the opposite direction and compresses the suspension in this area. The car's total weight isn't shifting, but the distribution of the car's weight is.

Acceleration and deceleration incorrectly applied cause disruption of motion. Downshifting causes rapid deceleration. The weight of the vehicle will shift in the direction of travel. For instance, navigating quickly around a corner will cause a vehicle to lean. This is called weight transfer. It is an internal force that disrupts motion. It is imperative to understand that any one of the eight factors can disturb the vehicle's motion. What makes it more dangerous is multiple factors being involved.

What a driver is controlling is kinetic energy.

- First, energy always goes in the direction of travel.

- Second, when a vehicle travels around a corner quickly, the vehicle will lean, called weight transfer.

- Third, when a driver slams on the brakes and creates a skid mark, kinetic energy exceeds the tires' surface grip. On ice and snow, one can never slam on the brakes without locking the vehicle up and creating an oversteer problem resulting in failure and instant loss of control of the vehicle.

- Keep in mind that oversteering can result in spinouts.

Two Types of Steering Control Problems
—Oversteer and Understeer

- **Oversteer** occurs when the rear wheels lose traction before the front wheels. The vehicle will turn more (sharper) than the driver intends because the tires have exceeded their surface grip. This often results in the truck spinning out. (Kinetic energy exceeds tire surface grip.) Contributing factors are over acceleration and weight transfer. It can also be caused by failing to brake correctly. The front stops faster than the rear.

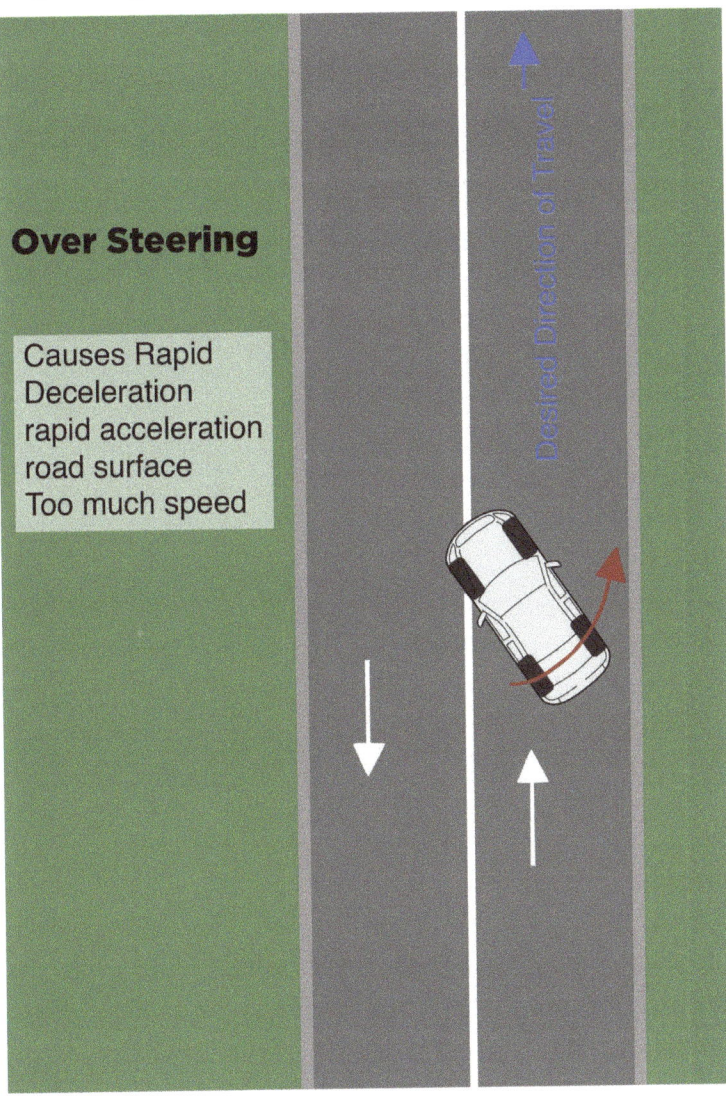

Over Steering

Causes Rapid
Deceleration
rapid acceleration
road surface
Too much speed

Desired Direction of Travel

- **Understeer** occurs when the front wheels lose traction before the rear wheels, and the driver can no longer turn the vehicle. The front tires lose their grip on the road, and the car turns less than commanded by the driver, resulting in the vehicle traveling wider than the intended path.

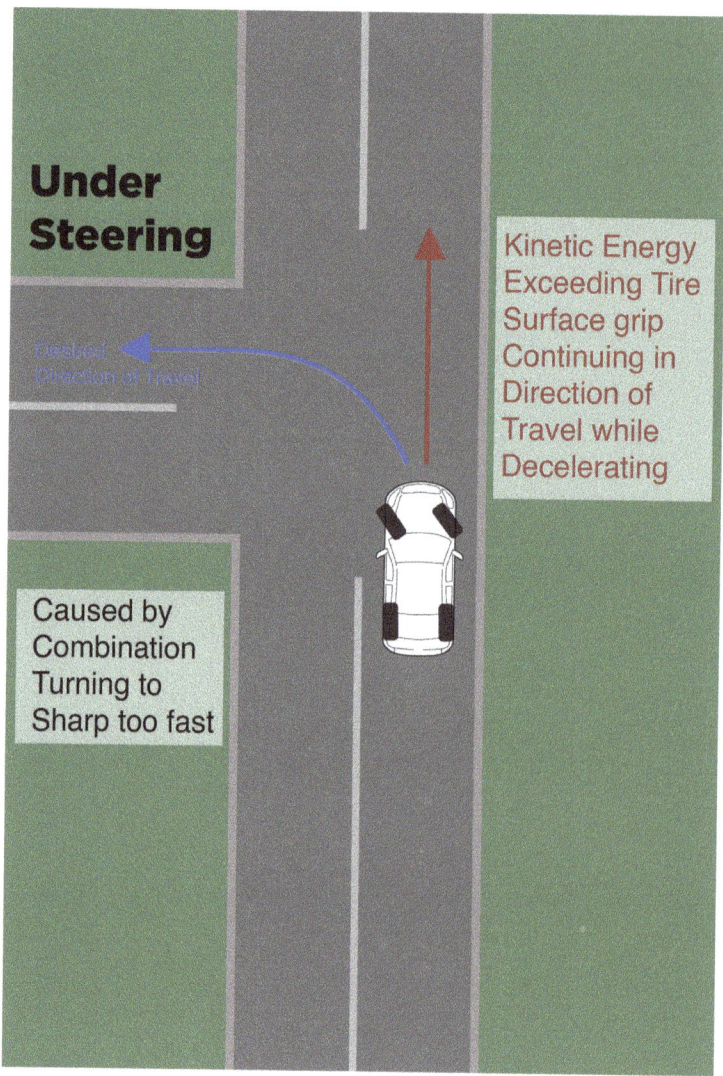

Breaking Done Correctly

A driver must apply the brakes subtly so that the vehicle's front does not stop faster than the vehicle's rear. Think of stepping on an eggshell. When a driver quickly stops, as much as 80% of the vehicle's weight can transfer to the front axle, thus creating a loss of friction on the rear surface. *All vehicles need time and space to stop safely.* The goal is to prevent a spin-out, which occurs when the front of a car/truck/tractor-trailer stops faster than the rear. Do *not* pump the brakes; instead, apply steady pressure. Pumping a vehicle's brakes can cause an abrupt disruption of motion, causing the front to stop faster than the rear. All braking while cornering is terrible. Therefore, the vehicle should roll slow enough through the corner not to cause a loss of control, which can result in a spinout.

Cornering Correctly

The forces involved in all cornering are weight transfer, speed, road surface, steering, and wind. Any one of these forces can affect a high-profile vehicle more than a low-profile vehicle in a corner. The driver must never forget to drive for the circumstances and conditions.

A driver should approach corners at a safe speed, one-half of the average traveling rate. For example, if a vehicle is traveling thirty miles per hour, then the vehicle should slow down to approximately half of that speed or fifteen miles per hour to navigate the corner safely. This safe action causes the vehicle not to lean or transfer any weight. Weight transfer in cornering will disrupt motion, causing the driver to lose control of the vehicle.

Remember to factor in the weather conditions when cornering. Steering on snow or ice incorrectly or too quickly will cause weight transfer of the vehicle to lean, causing a spin-out. Remember the rule of two: go slow enough into the corner and steer through the corner. This holds for passenger vehicles and tractor-trailers alike. You always want to avoid multiplying factors. You can be on ice or snow and safely brake and be on ice and snow and safely steer. Everything you do must be subtle, but never brake and steer and never accelerate and steer.

Also, remember that high-profile vehicles do not have equal traction because the front's weight is different from the rear; often, the front is heavier than the rear, such as vans.

Shifting

Shifting gears can affect a vehicle's surface grip. Just like steering and braking, shifting must be done subtly and smoothly.

Ice tip—use a higher gear on ice with low RPM. This will make over acceleration more difficult for manual transmissions.

Passing

Passing can be one of the most dangerous things a driver can do. When done incorrectly, acceleration and steering create an oversteer problem easily. The road surface is constantly changing. To safely pass, never want to steer and accelerate simultaneously. Instead, steer subtly, maintaining the same speed after the lane change is complete, and then accelerate slowly.

Passing tractor-trailers is inherently dangerous because the fast lane always tends to be the least used, and the surface can be much worse. Take caution traveling in the fast lane because the wheel tracks in the snow have more time to freeze. The fast lane is most often smoother because commercial motor vehicles, which usually travel in the slow lane, weight damages the road surface. However, the fast lane's surface is smoother, creating better grip, and it can be worse to travel on in rain, snow, or ice. Losing control of your vehicle while attempting to pass next to a tractor-trailer can be deadly for you and the tractor-trailer's occupants. If your vehicle hits the side of a tractor-trailer, the force of impact will double and can knock your car into the other lane or off the road.

The premium condition to pass is on a groomed road with a smooth, hard surface in a straight line with plenty of time to safely pass without overaccelerating

In the following video on YouTube, this very thing happens. Be forewarned that this video is quite graphic and shocking. https://youtu.be/UQRkEDFhtcQ

The Different Kinds of Propulsion Systems

As already mentioned, speed is one of the major contributing factors to people losing vehicle control. Learning time and space incorrectly, improper braking, and lane changes while traveling downhill and around corners are all things the driver needs to learn how to navigate correctly. All four kinds of vehicles should have traction devices in foul weather, and drivers should know how to use the devices. Over the years, I've met many drivers who had the devices in their vehicles, but they did not know how to install them.

All-Wheel and 4-Wheel Drives

All-Wheel and 4-Wheel drives are the best for winter driving, but they come with a problem —overconfident drivers who are more prone to driving fast because they believe their snow tires are all they need. While many All-Wheel and 4-Wheel drive owners are notorious for being overconfident, they lack the proper training in driving during inclement weather. In fact, Sierra Nevada tow truck drivers call 4-Wheel drives—the future tow. People believe that 4-Wheel and All-Wheel drives make driving in the mountains and on ice and snow safe, but like any tool, one needs to know how to use it.

Front-Wheel Drives

Front-Wheel drives can be great fuel savers, but they have pros and cons. Their light, short wheelbase makes it harder to control these vehicles, causing oversteer problems because drivers react too quickly. Additionally, the vehicles' lightweight causes them to have less surface grip. Front-Wheel drives do not have equal traction because their weight from the front is different from the rear.

Frozen road surfaces with various wheel tracks make it extremely hazardous to control Front-Wheel drives. Traction device laws require snow chains or cables to be installed on the front axles, which cause a hazard going downhill and around corners because the vehicle stops so quickly and so easily in the front, creating an oversteer problem. When a vehicle increases grip on the drive axle, it loses co-efficiency of friction. Think of it like this: friction is traction, and one wants to create equal friction as much as possible. The vehicle should also have chains or cables installed on the rear tires. Doing so will help the driver hold the road, so braking and cornering don't become a problem.

The safest traction device is studded tires on all four tires to create static rolling friction, making it safer and more challenging for the vehicle to break loose. I used them living in the

Sierra Nevadas. The following forces are involved in traction: weight transfer, road surface (which does not count in traction devices), speed due to gravity, braking, and steering.

Rear- or Two-Wheel Drives

Two-Wheel drives are most common in pickups and sports cars. Both vehicles are light in the rear and have powerful engines that can accelerate fast. These vehicles carry most of their weight in the front and are lighter in their rear. Many passenger pickups have added sandbags to their back beds to give them weight, which increases surface grip in the vehicle's rear. Traction devices go on the drive axle in the rear, helping make going downhill and around corners easier to control a Two-Wheel drive vehicle. Sports cars, however, should never get on the road in ice and snow. They are hazardous to themselves and others because they are so light and so fast.

Bridges and Overpasses

Factors with bridges and overpasses include speed, weight transfer, and road surface. Crossing a bridge or overpass with too much speed increases the bounce as the vehicle crosses over the expansion joint, the beginning of the bridge. When one's foot is on the gas pedal as the vehicle bounces, a fear-based response of over-acceleration happens, followed by panic braking resulting in a fatal loss of vehicle control.

To navigate bridges and overpasses correctly, the driver should complete the following:

- Approach at a safe speed. The lower the roll, the less the bounce.
- The driver should remove the foot from the throttle approaching the bridge, which doesn't disrupt the motion. In this case, only two forces are involved: road surface and weight transfer.
- The ground temperatures on bridges and highways are different for various reasons. The driver should err on the side of caution and anticipate that they are slick.

Steering, Braking, and Road Surface

Steering, braking, and the road surface can be three dangerous combinations and have caused many accidents.

Example: I was traveling westbound on I 80 from Reno, Nevada. I was almost at Boomtown, and the snow was around six inches deep and falling very heavily. Chain control was not up yet, as I was approaching where vehicles usually installed chains on the other side of the bridge. Visibility was very low when I noticed a pickup truck blocking my lane. He had lost control and had crashed into the bridge. No lights were on his vehicle even though the driver was still in the vehicle. The truck was white in color, making it even more challenging to see. I changed lanes quickly, losing control for a short moment. After I recovered and got around the vehicle, the truck behind me hit his brakes and crashed into the bridge and the pickup truck. I had maintained my two-factor rule (steering and road surface while on snow) and continued safely to my destination. Steering and braking are the most common mistakes made going around a corner where I was going straight and had to change lanes radically. Correctly counter steering time and space allowed me to gain control.

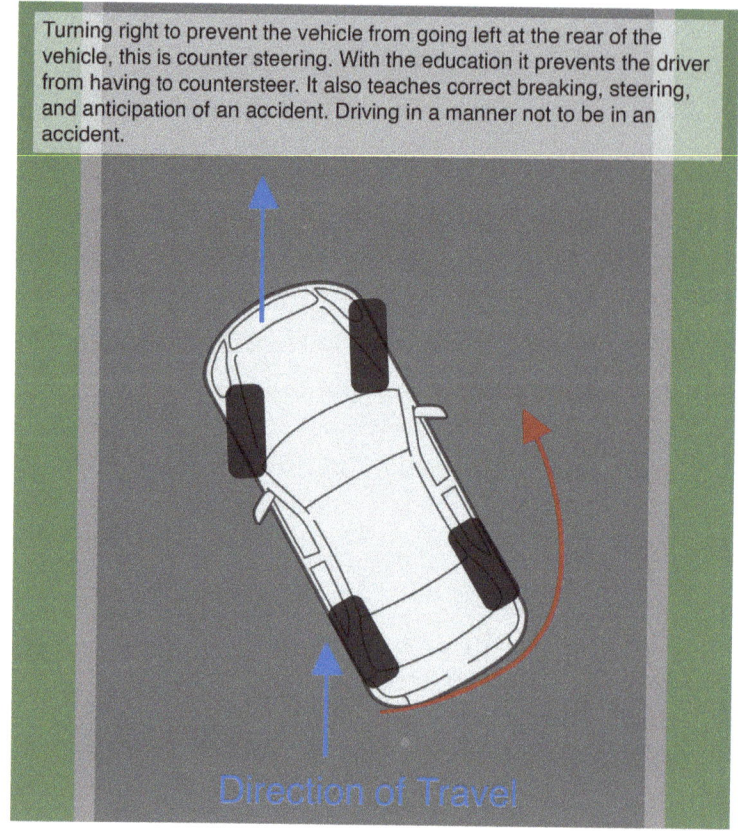

Turning right to prevent the vehicle from going left at the rear of the vehicle, this is counter steering. With the education it prevents the driver from having to countersteer. It also teaches correct breaking, steering, and anticipation of an accident. Driving in a manner not to be in an accident.

Direction of Travel

Remember the following dangerous combinations by themselves or together: over acceleration, road surface, and steering.

Degree of Fault Law

Degree of Fault Law, aka my Visual Driving Rule, is never to drive any faster than you can stop in half the distance that you can see. So, if you can see one mile ahead of you, you must be able to stop your vehicle fully within one-half mile. If your visibility is reduced, your ability to stop your car due to friction loss will also be reduced. Maintaining friction is necessary to control your vehicle.

Because I am always controlling my speed and distance, I am reducing my liability and chances of being in an accident. If the drivers in that I-81/Pennsylvania March 2022 wreck had used this rule and known how to brake correctly, more people would still be alive today, and most of those vehicles would not be wrecked. The Degree of Fault Law also allows for safe braking.

Anticipation Learning

How to anticipate an accident comes from knowing the Great Eight Forces or Factors and learning to recognize trouble spots, such as bridges, overpasses, corners, intersections, downhill corners, and blind spots in your path of travel. Be aware of multiplying forces, such as passing, by watching traffic and maintaining good space to give yourself increased time to brake to avoid others.

Additionally, watch for vehicles traveling too close to other vehicles and maintain a safe distance from cars that travel close together. Avoid "the pack" at all costs. For some reason, people always want to pack up, yet this is the greatest recipe for a chain reaction accident. Allow people to have room to make mistakes in front of you, so you reap the benefit of time and space to stop or go around the accident safely.

Learn the difference between a mistake and a lesson. A mistake gets repeated, and a lesson is learned by mistakes. Never take getting behind the wheel for granted.

Black Ice

Learning to predict black ice (sometimes called clear ice) isn't easy. Water freezes at 32° F. I use a laser thermometer to predict black ice to measure the ground temperature. The second thing I look at is dewpoint or moisture in the air. Any time there is more than 10° F, there is enough moisture in the air to create black ice. Other areas where you can observe signs of moisture are rivers, lakes, or creeks. Crossing bridges in the mountains can be especially dangerous because the ground temperature from the road temperature can be as much as 60° F different. After all, air can circulate above and below the bridge's surface.

Black ice is a thin layer of ice that reflects the color of the road. The ice itself is not black but visually transparent, allowing the often-black road below to be seen through it. Black ice is most prevalent during the morning hours, especially after snowmelt on the roadways has a chance to refreeze overnight when the temperature drops below 32° F. Black ice can also form when the roads are wet from rain and temperatures drop below 32° F.

Different regions around the North American continent can create different kinds of ice. The ice up north is pure, cold, and dry and practically freezes into a car's tires. The further south one goes, the wetter the ice becomes. All travel on ice is hazardous. People should not drive in icy conditions, especially if they're not trained. Because people take their driving skills for granted yet are untrained to handle an emergency with ice, they have a fear-based response, causing too many unnecessary accidents to occur every year.

In the winter of 2021, the people who lived in the Dallas-Fort Worth area heeded the advice and stayed off the icy roads. Yet as I traveled from Iowa to Fort Worth, Texas, I saw numerous four-wheel drives rolled over. The passenger vehicles were wise and stayed off the road, but the overconfident, untrained drivers in these four-wheel drives were littering the side of the road.

The Most Dangerous Roads
—Time to Chain-Up

The most dangerous roads are the roads between dry roads and chain control. Most wrecks happen because you do not have enough surface grip to run traction devices. However, after increasing the surface grip of your vehicle, your vehicle becomes much safer to drive.

So, consider this before you get on the road: stop, think, observe, and plan your goal. To get from point A to point B safely, ask yourself if the risk is worth the reward. Sometimes the best decision is to stay home if you don't know what you are doing. Because some truck drivers and drivers have been poorly trained, are over-confident in their driving skills, and have access to a poor chain product, they don't want to use snow chains. My rule is that if there are two or more inches of snow on the road, it is time to chain up. If there are wrecks in the chain control area, they are often caused by passenger vehicles losing control in front of tractor-trailers. The passenger vehicles were going too fast, and they didn't give themselves enough time and space to prevent the accident. You always want to drive as far away as you can from trucks and trailers.

Plan your route and check your weather and road conditions. Be aware of the dewpoint and ground temperature. *Windy* and *NOAA* weather apps are reliable apps to download. I also use the interstate web cameras to see in real-time the road conditions so that I can make good decisions. Be aware of high-profile vehicles in the wind, the ice, or the snow. Driving recreational vehicles such as camper trailers should not occur in those conditions.

Additionally, the same forces that contribute to wrecks in ice and snow will contribute to wrecks in the rain because the forces are the same, but the vehicle's velocity increases the impact.

- Respect the conditions and make good decisions.
- Keep a hot windshield with wet snow to prevent your wipers from freezing up.
- Keep them cold with powder snow. Cool windshields prevent the snow from melting on your wiper blades.
- *Rain X* helps prevent your glass from fogging up.
- Diesel-powered vehicles should carry products that prevent your diesel from gelling up.
- Keep food, water, and warm clothing with you if you break down. Snowstorms often delay tow trucks, so it could be a long time before you get help.

Rain and Multi-Ply Surfaces

Rain is an underestimated force, yet it will cause more havoc than ice or snow. Rain is statistically more dangerous than ice or snow because often greater speeds are involved. People tend to be more confident and drive faster, especially in Four-Wheel and All-Wheel drives in rainy conditions. Overconfidence is a killer because of these increased speeds on such a road surface. Automobile accidents are the number one killer of young people because of their ignorance of these facts.

Here are all the conditions that contribute to the dangers of driving in the rain:

- A wet road surface reduces friction; thus, caution must be taken on bridges, overpasses, and low-lying areas.

- Greater speeds increase the impact, increasing the possibility of death occurring.

- When visibility is reduced, never drive any faster than you can stop in half the distance that you can see. Statistics say the odds go up by 75% of being killed in a rainstorm. Visibility in the rain reduces the distance you can be seen and the distance a vehicle can stop due to the loss of friction. Maintaining frictions is vital to controlling a vehicle.

- Rain can also create glare to blind the driver as well as others. This same rule applies to fog.

Freezing fog, aka pogonip or tule fog, is the most hazardous. Pogonip is a fog consisting of fine ice suspended in the air in cold areas worldwide. This fog makes driving very dangerous because it can freeze a windshield, rapidly creating zero visibility. Maintaining all the heat on a windshield by pulling down the front visors helps trap the heat until the driver can safely get off the road. Remember, maintain a hot windshield in wet snow or ice and a cool windshield in dry powder snow.

To recap

- Don't brake and steer.
- Don't steer and accelerate.
- Remember the rule of 2.
- You can drive safely on snow if you know how to brake correctly.
- Don't multiply forces.
- Remember driving in ice and snow is a marathon, not a sprint; take your time.
- Don't drive if you don't have to

Glossary of Terms

- **Counter steering**: to counter an opposing force. It can steer tire blowout and oversteer problems but never multiply the force with braking. Allow the vehicle to slow down naturally. Do not apply the brake until the vehicle is at a low speed, under 15 mph.

- **Friction**: the resistance that one surface or object encounters when moving over another.

  o Coefficient of friction: a measure of the amount of resistance that a surface exerts on or substances moving over it, equal to the ratio of the maximal force that the surface exerts and the force pushing the object toward the surface.

  o Mechanical engineering: the force to move two sliding objects over each other. Divided by the force holding them together, it is a reduction once the motion has started.

- **Grade**: the measure of a road's steepness as it rises and falls along its route.

- **High-Profile**: any vehicle with a large, exposed surface area that crosswinds can affect (trucks, semis, some SUVs, etc.).

- **Kinetic energy**: a law of physics that says that a body possesses by being in motion.

- **Low-Profile**: any vehicle that has a small, exposed surface area that isn't impacted as much by wind (most cars).

- **Newton's Laws of Motion**: the three physical laws lay the foundation for classical mechanics. They describe the relationship between a body and the forces acting upon it and the motion in response to the forces.

  o The first law of motion states that a body remains at rest or in uniform motion in a straight line unless acted upon by force.

  o The second law of motion describes what happens to a massive body when acted upon by an external force. It states that the force acting on an object is equal to the mass of that object times its acceleration. (Simply put—it doubles its force upon impact.)

  o The third law of motion states there is an equal but opposite reaction for every action.

- **Road surface**: a road surface that is durable enough to sustain vehicle traffic.

- **Surface grip**: to seize or hold firmly

- **Forces That Disrupt Motion** (Internal) - Speed of rate at which someone or something moves.

  o Weight Transfer - A movement of weight from one side to another.

  o Aggressive Down Shifting Declaration - Reduction of speed or rate.

- o Acceleration - A vehicle's capacity to gain speed in a short time.
- o Steering - The action of steering a vehicle in a chosen direction of travel.

- External Forces that Disrupt Motion
  - o Wind - A natural current of air blowing from a particular direction.
  - o Road Surface - A road surface that is durable enough to sustain vehicle traffic.

Author's Note

I want to mention the people who supported, motivated, and sharpened me as a husband, father, professional driver, and author, starting with my beloved wife, Stacey Marie Martin. She has sacrificed more than anyone should have helped me make my dream come true.

I want to mention Richard and Pastor Cheryl Harper, my daughters, and their husbands. I am so grateful to Karen W. Dean for seeing the potential in my book and for offering her professional editing. An honorable mention, Marina Wood helped me gather the information for the snow training video, and Jessi and Kayla provided their typing skills, as we've only rewritten what seems like a million times. Thanks to a young couple, Bobby and Baylee, who exercised good decisions, hard work, and discipline at Jimmy's Egg in Midland, Texas. Thanks to my granddaughter, Taylor Kelley, for her computer skills; this has truly been a family endeavor.

And lastly, I want to give credit to someone who has learned the value of what this book teaches, Mason Griffin. His hard work and good discipline helped me solve the problems I had in creating this book.

I want to add the two worst decisions a person can make: (1) fail to train and (2) fail to know Jesus.

Sincerely,

Joe Martin

Excell PDT Professional Driving Training Quiz

1. What is kinetic energy?

   _____

2. Is kinetic energy subject to the laws of motions? Yes or No

3. What is the first thing kinetic energy does?

   _____

4. What is the second thing kinetic energy does?

   _____

5. How many external forces are there?

   _____

6. How many internal forces are there?

   _____

7. What is the rule of two?

   _____

8. What is the visual driving rule, aka the Degree of Fault rule?

   _____

9. The most dangerous road is between _____ and chain control.

10. Road temperature and _____ can vary as much as _____ degrees.

Excell PDT Professional Driving Training Quiz - Key

1. What is kinetic energy?
   Energy in motion or Energy that a body possesses by being in motion

2. Is kinetic energy subject to the laws of motions? Yes

3. What is the first thing kinetic energy does?
   Kinetic energy always moves in the direction of travel.

4. What is the second thing kinetic energy does?
   The second thing kinetic energy does is transfer weight in the corner.

5. How many external forces are there? 2 (two)

6. How many internal forces are there? 6 (six)

7. What is the rule of two?
   The rule of two is never to go over two forces or factors.

8. What is the visual driving rule, aka the Degree of Fault rule?
   The visual driving, aka Degree of Fault, rule states you should never drive any faster than you can stop in half the distance that you can see.

9. The most dangerous road is between dry road and chain control.

10. Road temperature and ground temperature can vary as much as 60 degrees.